Ravensburger Taschenbücher
Band 561

Wolfgang Ecke

The Man in Black

and other detective stories

Otto Maier Verlag Ravensburg

Hinweis

Schwierige Vokabeln werden nur beim ersten Auftreten in den Fußnoten unten auf der Seite aufgeführt, ansonsten im alphabetischen Gesamtverzeichnis. Andere Vokabeln sind nur im alphabetischen Gesamtverzeichnis am Schluß des Buches zu finden. Es empfiehlt sich also, häufiger dort nachzuschlagen.

Erstmals 1979 in den Ravensburger Taschenbüchern

Titel der englischen Ausgabe:
"Be A Super Sleuth with the Case of the Face at the Window"

Englische Übersetzung: Stella und Vernon Humphries
Die Geschichten sind erstmals in folgenden
Ravensburger Taschenbüchern auf deutsch erschienen:
Band 208 Das Schloß der roten Affen
Band 214 Der Mann in Schwarz
Band 221 Das Gesicht an der Scheibe
Bearbeitung: Uwe Lüer

Illustrationen: Rolf Rettich
Umschlaggestaltung: Graphisches Atelier Otto Maier Verlag,
unter Verwendung einer Zeichnung von Rolf Rettich

Satz: IBV Lichtsatz KG, Berlin
Druck und Verarbeitung: Ebner Ulm

9 8 7 6 5 88 87 86 85 84

ISBN 3-473-39561-7

Contents

Solutions: ⋆easy

⋆⋆quite difficult

⋆⋆⋆difficult

1 The man in black

His beard was black and bushy, his glasses had gold rims and he wore a grey suit. His room was one of the cheaper ones at the Savoyard, a small old hotel whose outside plaster was flaking away year by year.

For half an hour now he had been walking up and down his room, staring impatiently at the telephone every few minutes. At last, at half past six in the evening, it rang. "Hello!" he whispered.

The voice that answered was no louder than the first speaker's but less friendly. "Georges, it's me. Just to say that it's OK for tonight. I've prepared things as we arranged. Go to the sixth floor in the staff lift, and when you get out you'll see a fire extinguisher beside it. The key to 613 is fixed to the back of it with a piece of sticky tape. The things you need are in the cupboard there and the rope-

---

rim	– Rand
suit	– Anzug
plaster	– Gips, Außenputz
to flake away	– abblättern
impatient	– ungeduldig
staff lift	– Personalaufzug
fire extinguisher	– Feuerlöscher
to fix	– befestigen
sticky tape	– Klebeband
rope-ladder	– Strickleiter

ladder will reach down to the fourth floor. The best time, I'd say, is between two and three. Is everything clear?"

A fleeting smile played round Georges' lips. "Yes, perfectly. And what will you be doing, Pierre, while I'm hard at work?"

"I'm glad to say I'm being sent to Cannes and I shan't be back till tomorrow morning. And I hope more than I can say that I'll never see you again."

A click informed the man with the beard that the speaker had rung off. Georges did the same.

That night was moonless. A warm air lay over the whole of the French Riviera. In St Tropez the usual lively parties were still in full swing. The roulette wheels were still spinning merrily in Nice and Monte Carlo. But Antibes had become an oasis of peace and quiet. Along the seafront the few remaining lights in the big hotels were going out one by one.

At exactly twenty past two a window on the sixth floor of the Hotel Europa was warily pushed open. A man leaned out and looked down at the front

---

to reach	– reichen; erreichen
fleeting	– flüchtig
to ring off	– auflegen
in full swing	– in vollem Gang
to spin	– sich drehen
remaining	– verbleibenden
warily	– vorsichtig, behutsam
to lean out	– sich hinauslehnen

of the building. He wore black overalls, a dark mask and gloves. After a moment or so he began lowering a rope-ladder. With the utmost caution, avoiding any sideways movement, he let the ladder down until it came to rest just above the balcony of a room on the fourth floor.

Again the man leaned out of the window and looked down. For a few seconds he remained there, motionless.

Somewhere in the town a clock struck the half hour. As if at a signal, the masked figure jumped on the window sill blocking the window opening. But not for long: his feet found the springy rungs and he climbed down the rope-ladder as nimbly as a circus performer.

Once past the open window of Room 513 on the fifth floor he quickly reached the balcony of 413 on the floor below. As he stepped down, he saw that the French windows were wide open and the

---

gloves	– Handschuhe
to lower	– herunterlassen
caution	– Vorsicht
to avoid	– vermeiden
sideways movement	– Bewegung zur Seite
motionless	– bewegungslos
springy	– federnd, elastisch
rung	– Sprosse
nimbly	– gewandt, geschickt
circus performer	– Artist
once past...	– nachdem er einmal vorbei war an...
French window	– Verandatür

curtains were moving in the soft breeze.
The masked man held his breath, listening, and he only relaxed when he heard faint snores from within the room. He knew that Signor Ettore Sartoni from Florence was in a deep sleep.
Carefully the man drew aside the curtain.
When he stepped out again, only four minutes had passed. He hardly paused before swinging himself over the balcony and on to the next one, where he repeated his performance in even less time. And not only there... His further visits to other bedrooms were not entirely fruitless...
If people don't enjoy breakfast, it's probably because they've slept badly. But if some of the Hotel Europa's guests failed to enjoy their first meal that next morning it was not so much because of a restless night as because of the discoveries they made after waking up.
Miss Gloria Tucker from Boston, Massachusetts,

---

breeze	– Brise, sanfter Wind
held his breath	– hielt seinen Atem an
to relax	– sich entspannen; hier: wieder atmen
faint snores	– schwache Schnarchgeräusche
to repeat	– wiederholen
performance	– Werk, Tat
further	– weitere
entirely fruitless	– gänzlich nutzlos
probably	– vermutlich
fail to enjoy	– keinen Gefallen finden an
restless	– ruhelos
discoveries	– Entdeckungen

was the first to burst into the foyer with tears streaming down her face. She seized Monsieur Hector, the manager, by the lapels as she sobbed out her story.

Hard on her heels came Ettore Sartoni, a jeweller from Florence, followed by a retired general from Bulgaria, Serge Balinoff. Their losses were enormous, and Monsieur Hector's face grew paler and paler. His small hands went nervously up and down and his Adam's apple rose and fell with the report of each new disaster. By the time the Aurillacs came tottering out of the lift the manager knew that he now had to take action. Balancing from foot to foot like a flamingo, he teetered his way across the hall to the reception desk and, reaching for the telephone, in a faint voice he asked for the police.

That same afternoon, at about five o'clock, there

---

to burst into	– hereinstürmen
tear	– Träne
to seize	– packen, (er)greifen
lapel	– Rockaufschlag
to sob out	– hinausseufzen
jeweller	– Juwelier
retired	– pensioniert
loss	– Verlust
pale	– blaß
disaster	– Katastrophe
to totter	– torkeln, schwanken
to take action	– handeln
to teeter	– wanken, schaukeln
reception desk	– Empfang(sschalter)

was a knock at Perry Clifton's door.
Perry Clifton, the famous detective, was spending a holiday at Antibes. He had just returned from a long hot afternoon on the beach and was stretched out comfortably on his bed.
"Come in!" he called, slightly annoyed at being disturbed, but also curious as to the identity of the visitor.
"Do forgive me, Mr Clifton. My name is Michel Dumont. I'm sorry to disturb you, but I wonder if you can possibly spare a few moments for a colleague in need of your help?"
Perry Clifton jumped to his feet, amused. "There must be some mistake, Monsieur. I think you've come to the wrong floor."
Michel Dumont was clearly puzzled. "Aren't you Mr Perry Clifton?"
"I am."
"The detective from London?"
This time it was Perry's turn to look surprised. "Yes, but I didn't think anyone here in Antibes knew about me or what I do."

---

comfortably	– bequem
slightly annoyed	– leicht verärgert
to disturb	– stören
curious as to	– neugierig in Bezug auf
identity	– Identität, wer jemand ist
to wonder	– wissen mögen
to spare	– erübrigen, übrig haben
it was Perry's turn	– P. war an der Reihe

"If it will put your mind at rest, I'll tell you that a certain Mr Pickles who often stays here told me who you are."
Perry Clifton searched his memory. "Pickles? I remember having heard this name..."
Dumont came to help him. "He's a big shot in one of the insurance companies in the City..."
"Of course, that's it!" exclaimed Clifton. "He has a dog he calls Horatio. In fact, it was a case with the dog that brought us together."
"Small world, isn't it?"
The Englishman nodded. "You started by asking me if I could spare a moment for a professional colleague. So I'm right to say that you're a detective, too?"
"Yes, I'm the house detective here at the Europa. And, to tell you the truth, it's a job with more headaches than rewards," said Dumont grimly.
"Oh come, Monsieur Dumont," smiled Perry. "Being here on the Riviera, with the sunshine, white sands, blue skies and even bluer sea – to say nothing of all these charming rich people... isn't that worth something?"

---

to put at rest	– beruhigen
to search	– (durch)suchen
a big shot	– „großes Tier", Bonze
insurance company	– Versicherungsgesellschaft
truth	– Wahrheit
headaches	– Kopfweh; Kummer
reward	– Belohnung, Erfolg

"These charming rich people, as you call them, are the cause of all the trouble," said Dumont.
"I understand. But what is it I can do for you?"
Michel Dumont did not beat about the bush. "I need someone's help," he answered, "and there's no one else I can ask."
"But how can I possibly help you?"
"You know about last night, I think?"
Perry nodded. "I heard that some rooms were burgled, and when I came in a short time ago I saw that the entrance hall was full of policemen."
"Ah yes," muttered Dumont. "Our splendid local policemen! What happened last night was that a cat burglar took advantage of the warm night and open doors and windows to drop in on some of our wealthiest guests – and with enormous success from his point of view, it seems. Since ten o'clock this morning the police have been in and out, cross-examining everyone. You will be one of the next, I think, Mr Clifton."
The French detective walked slowly to the window

---

cause	– Grund, Ursache
beat about the bush	– um den heißen Brei herumreden
to burgle	– bestehlen
to mutter	– murmeln
local	– örtlich, Orts-
	– Fassadenkletterer, Einsteigdieb
	– seinen Nutzen ziehen aus
	– jemand überraschend besuchen
	– wohlhabend
	– ins Kreuzverhör nehmen

and looked out. As he turned back to Perry, his voice had a defiant ring to it. "I have to confess that Inspector Mellier and I can't be called friends; he doesn't think much of me as a detective. Well, I'd like to show him this time that I've got the better nose, and that I can solve the case first."
By now, Perry Clifton, who had been listening attentively, looked much more eager to co-operate. "So far so good. Only how do you think I can help you? Are there any hard facts to start with?"
The hotel detective beamed with delight. He seized Clifton's hand and shook it warmly. "I knew it!" he exclaimed. "I knew you wouldn't let me down. Of course there are facts and, indeed, there are quite a lot. Some that Mellier knows, and some that only I know."
"Let's begin with the first ones."
"The investigations so far show clearly that the thief was operating between two and three this morning. He let down a rope-ladder from an

---

a defiant ring	– einen trotzigen Unterton
confess	– bekennen, zugeben
to solve	– lösen
case	– Fall
attentive	– aufmerksam
eager	– begierig
co-operate	– zusammenarbeiten
to beam with delight	– vor Freude strahlen
to exclaim	– ausrufen
to let down	– allein lassen, enttäuschen
investigation	– Untersuchung

unused staff bedroom on the sixth floor, that is from Room 613. We found the ladder in the cupboard. It was just long enough to reach the fourth floor which is the only floor with balconies.
"The burglar must have climbed down and landed on the balcony of Suite 413, which is occupied by a certain Signor Ettore Sartoni, a jeweller from Florence. I'm afraid he's about 70,000 Francs the poorer since last night.
"The next of our guests whom that fellow paid a visit was a Swiss lady, Frau Treicher. She's said to be extremely rich, and owns a few hotels herself. She, too, lost a considerable sum. On the fifth floor, the American young lady, Miss Tucker, was the first victim. According to her, the burglar made off with a jewel case whose contents were worth 120,000 Francs.
"Next to her is a retired Bulgarian general who has just sold his memoirs for a princely sum. He came here telling everybody that he intended to spend it all, and now it looks as though he'll have no

---

unused staff bedroom	– unbenutztes Zimmer eines Hausangestellten
to occupy	– belegen, bewohnen
jeweller	– Juwelier
he's about ... the poorer	– er ist um .... ärmer
to pay a visit	– einen Besuch abstatten
to own	– besitzen
considerable	– beträchtlich
victim	– Opfer

problems in that respect."
"Anyone else?"
"Oh yes. There are the Aurillacs from Paris in the room next to the General's. Madame's jewellery and Monsieur's wallet are both missing."
"Quite a greedy fellow, isn't he?" interjected Perry Clifton.
"You can say that again! The last victim was Mr Stan Simpson from Texas. He's in the room below Frau Treicher's. Mr Simpson said, the fellow disappeared with 20,000 Dollars and a precious cigarette case."
Perry Clifton shook his head. "I can never understand why rich people carry all that valuable stuff around with them... One question, though, Monsieur Dumont. If only the fourth-floor rooms have balconies, how could the man come and go so easily in and out of the fifth-floor windows?"
"There's a broad ledge that runs all round the building just below the fifth-floor windows. It's like a balcony for an expert cat burglar."
"So, altogether, six guests have been robbed." Perry Clifton summed up the position so far. "And

---

in that respect	– in dieser Hinsicht
wallet	– Brieftasche
greedy	– gierig
to interject	– einwerfen, unterbrechen
precious	– wertvoll
ledge	– Sims

three of them have rooms on the fifth floor?"
"Yes. You can imagine the situation in which the management is. Then along come the police, interfering, rushing about with all the tact of a charging rhinoceros, and still completely in the dark as to who could have done it. It so happens that all the well-known cat burglars who might tackle this kind of job have already been arrested. The culprit might be someone living in the hotel, but it could just as well be a fellow from outside."
"So much for the facts that you and Inspector Mellier know. But what else have you found out, Monsieur Dumont? Let me see your trump card!"
Although Michel Dumont again looked slightly embarrassed, he quickly recovered his self-possession. "I may not know if the burglar is living here or not," he explained, "but I believe an accomplice of his has a room in the hotel."
"And is this person a man with a name, or is it only a guess?"
"His name is Pierre Bassu. He's an assistant chef and like several of the staff – me too, by the way

---

to interfere	– sich einmischen
tact of a charging rhinoceros	– Feingefühl eines angreifenden Rh.
to tackle	– in Angriff nehmen, wagen
culprit	– Übeltäter, Schuldiger
embarrassed	– verwirrt
to recover the selfpossession	– die Fassung wiederfinden
accomplice	– Komplize
assistant chef	– stellvertr. Küchenchef

– he has a room on the sixth floor. Yesterday, quite by chance, I noticed Bassu coming out of Room 613, but he didn't notice me. Now I ask you, Mr Clifton, what was he doing in that room, which is unoccupied at present?"

"Room 613, eh? That's the one where you said the rope-ladder was found. Yes, you're right. That seems very odd."

"Bassu could certainly have left the rope-ladder there for an accomplice. And I should also tell you that this is Bassu's first season on the Hotel Europa's staff."

"That in itself wouldn't be suspicious," said Perry Clifton thoughtfully.

But Dumont raised his hand. "Let me finish. According to his papers, he used to work at the Hotel Tunese in Paris, but when I tried to get information about him there..."

Clifton leaned forward. "Yes? What was the result?"

"It was most interesting. A Hotel Tunese doesn't exist. There's no such hotel in and around Paris."

"Well, well. You've already succeeded, Monsieur

---

quite by chance	– ganz zufällig
odd	– komisch, eigenartig
suspicious	– verdächtig
to lean forward	– sich vorbeugen
result	– Ergebnis
to succeed	– Erfolg haben

Dumont. What more do you want? All you have to do is to turn Inspector Mellier loose on this Bassu."

"No, no," said the Frenchman, shaking his head, "I don't want a half victory. And that's what it would be if it turns out that Pierre Bassu is no more than a minor accomplice. It can't have been Bassu himself, you see. From yesterday afternoon until this morning, the management had sent him as relief chef to our sister hotel, the Royale in Cannes. Now it was here where I hoped for your help, Mr Clifton. I want to ask if you couldn't try and get the truth out of Bassu. You see, he knows who I am here and therefore he'll be on his guard against me, but you..."

Perry Clifton couldn't help grinning. "In other words, you want me to pretend to Bassu that I'm a fellow crook? But what if he sees the trick?"

"Well, there are only two alternatives. Either he's involved, then perhaps he'll own up. Or he's com-

---

to turn loose on	– auf die Fährte setzen
minor	– gering, unbedeutend
to turn out	– sich herausstellen
relief-	– Aushilfs-
to be on the guard	– auf der Hut sein
to pretend	– vortäuschen, so tun als ob
crook	– hier: Gauner, Betrüger
fellow crook	– konkurrierender Gauner, hier: Rivale
to involve	– verwickeln, beteiligen
to own up	– ein Geständnis ablegen

pletely innocent, and then he'll be the first to call for help."

"And I'll find myself in a very tricky situation," said Clifton.

"I'll be at hand, I promise. I'll come to your assistance if you need me."

"Very well! When should I call on the gentleman?"

Dumont thought for a moment. "Bassu is off duty between six and eight this evening. He usually spends his free time alone in his room. I suggest you go and see him then."

It was exactly seven o'clock.

Perry Clifton tapped on the door of Room 642 and waited. He was wearing a hat pulled down over his forehead and dark glasses. In the corner of his mouth he held a matchstick.

"Come in!" said a sleepy voice from the other side of the door. The English detective entered, closed the door softly behind him and leaned against it. "Evening, Pierre!" he murmured and scowled at the man on the bed.

Pierre Bassu was a thin man of about forty. He got

---

innocent	– unschuldig
to call on somebody	– bei jemand vorsprechen
off duty	– dienstfrei
to tap	– klopfen
to scowl at	– finster anblicken

up slowly and looked at his visitor with a weary expression, which changed first to one of embarrassment and then to one of rage. "What do you want?" he cried hoarsely.
Perry spat out the match and with one finger he pushed his hat back and replied quietly. "Don't you remember me, Pierre? I'm Tommy from London. You can tell me by my accent, can't you? Well? Hasn't the penny dropped yet?" Clifton did not give the man time to reply, but went on remorselessly: "You've messed things up for me very nicely, I must say. That business with the rope-ladder is my speciality, remember? I'd got it all worked out and I was waiting for the right moment. Why else would I be living in a posh joint like this?"
There was something menacing in his voice, and he stared at Bassu through his sunglasses.
Bassu swallowed hard and began stammering: "It's j... j... just as I thought. You're mi... mi... mixing me up with someone else, sir..."

---

weary	– müde
rage	– Wut
hoarse	– heiser
the penny drops	– der Groschen fällt
remorseless	– erbarmungslos
to mess up	– „versauen", durcheinanderbringen
posh joint	– pikfeiner „Laden", Lokal, Hotel
to menace	– drohen
to swallow	– schlucken
to stammer	– stammeln
to mix up with	– verwechseln mit

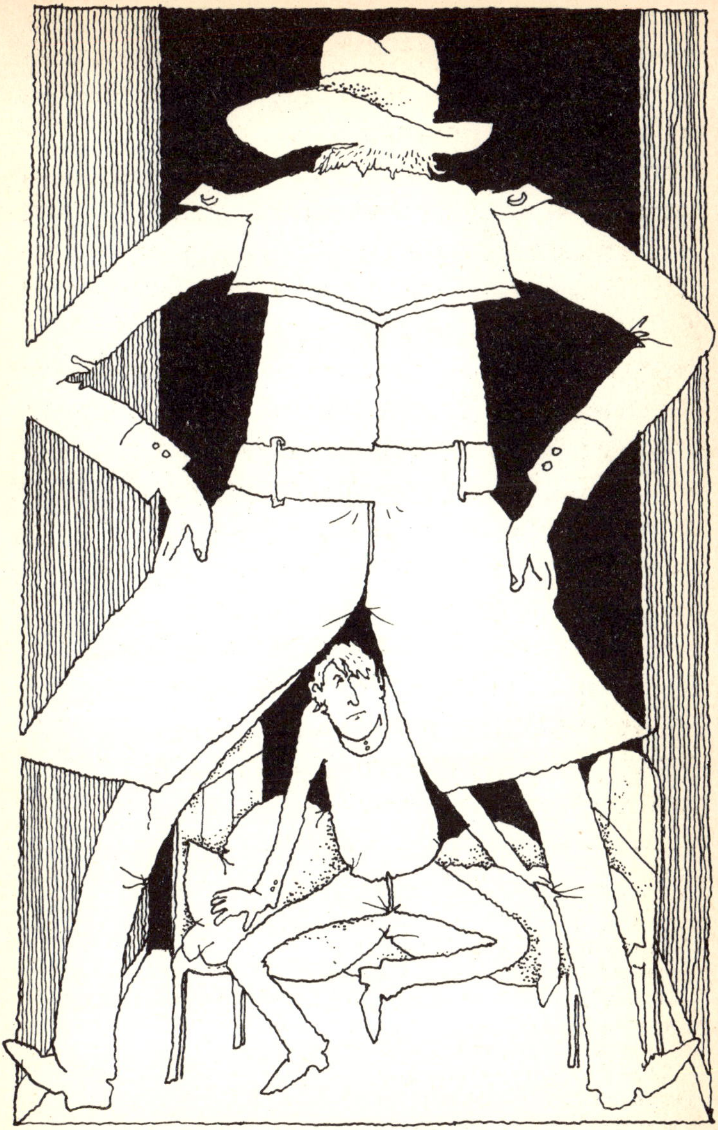

"Am I really? I'm mixing you up with another fellow?"
"That's right, sir. I've nothing to do with this robbery."
"What a laugh! There's a burglary at the hotel, and our dear friend Pierre has nothing to do with it!"
Again Bassu swallowed. He was in a state of panic and his voice had grown even hoarser than before.
"I wasn't even in the hotel last night," he protested.
As Perry stepped forward, Bassu immediately stepped back, so that the distance between the two men remained the same. The Frenchman looked to the door.
Clifton saw this and said sarcastically: "It's not very nice out there on the landing, Pierre. The police are waiting for you. Tell me now…"
Bassu didn't let him finish his sentence. "I'm not afraid of the police," he interrupted with more haste than conviction.
"What? Have I really made a mistake?"
"Yes, you have. I told you so right away, sir," replied the man with returning hope.
"Now I'm completely mystified. Just imagine,

---

to remain – bleiben
landing – Treppenabsatz
haste – Eile
conviction – Überzeugung
mystified – verwirrt; hinters Licht geführt

Pierre. I could have sworn you were the chef I knew in Paris. Why, he's your double..."
"It c... c... can happen sometimes," stammered Pierre, calculating the distance to the door. But Clifton would not let him off so easily.
"I really took you for a man who did the cooking at the Hotel Tunese... such a coincidence."
Bassu's face turned white like chalk and he was terrified out of his wits as he dropped back on the bed, while Clifton continued: "Why aren't you working in Paris, these days? You had a wonderful job at the Tunese."
"How is it you know so much about me?" whispered Bassu, his voice so weak that Perry felt almost sorry for the man. He decided not to prolong the agony.
"Come on, Bassu. I'll give you one more chance. Tell me the name of the cat burglar and I promise to keep your name out of it when I report to Inspector Mellier. Is that OK? Out with it!"
Pierre Bassu sat on his bed, and stared in front of him, resigned. His voice was almost hopeless. "So you're not a crook. You're from the police... I knew there'd be trouble... But Georges Bardin had me in the hollow of his hand."

---

coincidence – Zusammentreffen; Zufall
terrified out of his wits – zu Tode erschrocken
to prolong the agony – die Qual verlängern
in the hollow of the hand – völlig in der Gewalt

"Did he blackmail you?"

"Yes. I had been in jail and when I came out there was nobody who dared to give me a job. It was Bardin who got me false papers. And I soon discovered why he was so keen to help me. Suddenly he turned up here in Antibes, and threatened me that he'd tell the management about my past if I didn't help him... What could I do, sir?"

Bassu's story aroused Clifton's interest. He took off his sunglasses and his hat. "Now I'll try to help you. So the thief's name is Georges Bardin. And where can we find him?"

"He has a room at the Savoyard Hotel."

Clifton's hand was already on the door-handle. "Thank you for your valuable assistance, Monsieur Bassu. For the time being, please behave as if nothing has happened..."

When Michel Dumont came into the room he was carrying two glasses and a bottle of champagne. Clifton welcomed him enthusiastically. "From your festive preparations I guess you've caught

---

to blackmail	– erpressen
to discover	– entdecken
keen	– begierig, eifrig
to threaten	– drohen
to arouse	– erwecken
valuable	– wertvoll
to behave	– sich verhalten; betragen
festive	– feierlich, festlich

your fish safely?"
"Yes, indeed, Mr Clifton. He was arrested fifteen minutes ago. Inspector Mellier couldn't believe his eyes and ears. He bombarded me with questions, but I only smiled and muttered something about having 'various contacts, you know'! By the way, you were quite right. Bardin immediately tried to put the blame on Bassu, as you said he would."
"What will happen to Bassu, poor fellow?"
"You needn't feel too worried about him, you know. It's going to be all right. Mellier questioned him, of course, but he's been let off with a caution. And the management here has no objection to his remaining on the staff."
"I'm delighted to hear it. But what about the stolen goods though? Have they all been recovered yet?"
"Yes, I think so. Bardin hadn't time to get rid of them. We found everything in the false bottom of a trunk in Bardin's room. But what's so amusing about that?"
"I'm trying to imagine the expression on some-

---

by the way	– nebenbei bemerkt
to put the blame on	– die Schuld schieben auf
to let off with a caution	– mit einer Verwarnung davonkommen lassen
objection	– Einwand
to get rid of	– loswerden
trunk	– großer Koffer
expression	– (Gesichts-)Ausdruck

one's face when it becomes known that the thief has been arrested and the stuff recovered, too."
"I don't understand what you mean, Mr Clifton. What expression do you expect?"
"One of shock... or even alarm."
"I still don't understand..."
"Then I'll explain. Of Bardin's six victims, one will be very scared – the one who was telling lies."
"Are you saying...?" Michel Dumont struggled for words. "But that's impossible!"
"No, it isn't. Don't you remember my saying: 'All these charming rich people!'? But it may console you to know that even they sometimes try to defraud insurance companies..."
Dumont shook his head, puzzled. "But which of them is it? And how on earth did you find out?"
"Simply from your description of the so-called victims. I'm sure you can work it out for yourself. It's not so difficult. All you have to do is follow the footsteps of the cat burglar! Your very good health, Monsieur Dumont!"

Which of the hotel's guests had made a false statement about being robbed?

---

to struggle for	– ringen nach
to console	– trösten
to defraud	– betrügen
your very good health!	– auf Ihre Gesundheit!
statement	– Aussage

2 The rehearsal

It was shortly after nine o'clock that the last member of the orchestra arrived at Philharmonia Hall on the morning of the gala concert. It was, as usual, Arnold Stone, the flute-player. In the doorway he almost collided with a young man wearing a black and yellow sports jacket, who seemed to be in a great hurry. Arnold Stone still found time to say "Good morning" to the friendly commissionaire Mr Hart, and although he could hear the string players already tuning up in the first-floor rehearsal-room he didn't quicken his steps.

Arnold Stone was the kind of person who always turned up late for appointments. But as he was a really outstanding flutist, the conductor, Mr Block, was good enough to overlook his being late. In no time at all Arnold had taken his place and the rehearsal could begin.

At exactly twelve the rehearsal was over. A few

---

rehearsal	– (Orchester-)Probe
to collide	– zusammenstoßen
commissionaire	– Portier
string player	– Spieler eines Streichinstruments
to tune up	– stimmen
to quicken	– beschleunigen
outstanding	– hervorragend
conductor	– Dirigent

moments later, the small cloakroom was crowded with members of the orchestra all talking and trying to find their coats. Suddenly there was a sharp, bewildered cry from the oboeist, Max Brand. "My briefcase has disappeared!" he shouted.

Immediately there was total silence. Then the others hastily inspected their various belongings – and with devastating results. Thirty-nine musicians found that money had been taken from their coats, and a few of the missing sums were quite considerable. Everyone was horrified.

Mr Block, the conductor, was the only one to keep his head. "Gentlemen, please, don't panic, I beg you! Just stay where you are for a moment!" he cried, trying to restore order. And to the caretaker, Mr Corbett he said: "Will you please fetch the commissionaire?".

A little later, Alfred Hart stood in front of the conductor. When he was told what had happened, the commissionaire turned pale with shock and

---

cloakroom – Garderobe
bewildered – bestürzt
briefcase – Aktentasche
various belongings – verschiedene Habseligkeiten
devastating – verheerend
considerable – beträchtlich
horrified – entsetzt
to keep one's head – einen kühlen Kopf behalten
caretaker – Verwalter, Aufseher, Notenwart

groped for a chair.
"Haven't you seen anyone, Mr Hart?" said Mr Block.
The doorman shook his head. "This is terrible, simply terrible," he moaned. "I haven't seen a soul, really I haven't. I've been downstairs the whole morning." Then his eye caught sight of the flute-player. "You were the last to arrive, weren't you, Mr Stone?"
The flutist gasped, and for one little moment it

---

to grope for	– tasten nach
to moan	– stöhnen, klagen
to gasp	– nach Luft schnappen

looked as if he were going to attack the commissionaire. "Do you mean that I...?"
"Gentlemen, please, a little self-control!" the conductor intervened.
Stone stepped back and patted his hair nervously. "Perhaps you want to have a look into my pockets?" he asked ironically. Then he remembered something. "Wait a minute, Mr Hart," he said, pointing a finger at the commissionaire. "When I arrived this morning I almost collided in the doorway with a young man. He was just leaving, and in a great hurry, too. Who was he?"
Mr Hart frowned and then clapped a hand to his forehead. "Of course," he exclaimed. "Why didn't I think of him before! It could easily have been him. He came from the music publishers to deliver some scores. I wondered why he was so long in the cloakroom, searching among the coats and even picking up people's hats."
"What? He was searching among the coats?" asked the conductor, appalled.
"Yes. He said he was looking for his scarf, but I realize now what a thin excuse that was!"

---

to intervene	– dazwischentreten
to pat	– hier: streichen über
to frown	– die Stirn runzeln
music publishers	– Musikverlag
to deliver	– abgeben
scores	– Partituren, Noten
appalled	– entsetzt
thin excuse	– dürftige Entschuldigung

The conductor turned to the caretaker. "Phone the police, Mr Corbett. They'd better find out more about this young man."
"Certainly, sir. I'll do it right away."
"I'll come with you," announced Arnold Stone, who had recovered his self-control. Turning to the others, he said in an offhand voice: "I'm in a hurry. Besides, nothing of mine was stolen. See you all this evening. Goodbye."

Who stole the money from the cloakroom?

---

offhand – kurz angebunden

3 Grimble is daft!

When Mr Grimble entered the classroom that Friday morning he stopped as if rooted to the spot. For there on the blackboard in huge red letters were written the words *Grimble is daft!*
Mr Grimble thought for a moment. This could only have been the work of one of the four boys who had been kept in after school on the day before. And they were Gerald Fink, Alex White, Michael Cash and Laurie Upton.
Mr Grimble turned the blackboard round so that its unfriendly remark could not be seen, and he settled down to have a look at some books. Half an hour later, when the first of the eleven-year-olds arrived, Mr Grimble did not look up.
Then lessons began. The first three of them passed without anything special happening. It was just like any other day. But when the bell rang for break, Mr Grimble told the whole class to wait while we wrote four names on the board: Fink, White, Cash and Upton. Then he said: "I want these four to remain behind. Into the playground with the rest of you."

---

daft	– doof, blöd
rooted to the spot	– angewurzelt
to keep in	– zum Nachsitzen dabehalten

The four boys came to the blackboard and assumed their most angelic expressions. "One of you has written a most impertinent remark on the other side of the blackboard," he thundered. "Which of you did it?"
The four boys huddled closer, afraid of what was to come.
"Was it you, Gerald?"
Fink shook his head energetically. "No, it's not me, sir," he assured the teacher with a most sincere look in his wide eyes.
"What have you to say, Alex?"
"I don't know anything about it, sir," protested Alex, and his ears turned red.
Michael Cash had a bright idea. "Perhaps someone broke in during the night," he said. "And when he saw the lovely red chalk lying there..."
"Is that the best thing you can think of, Cash?" asked the teacher in his most withering tone.
"I only thought..."
"And what about you, Laurence?"
Upton scratched his nose and said rather uncon-

---

to assume	– annehmen, ‚aufsetzen'
angelic expression	– Engelsgesicht, Unschuldsmiene
impertinent	– unverschämt
to huddle	– sich zusammendrängen
to assure	– versichern
sincere	– ernst
withering	– vernichtend, streng
to scratch	– kratzen
unconvincing	– ohne Überzeugung

vincingly: "I didn't do it, sir. I don't even know what it says on the board."
Mr Grimble shook his head. "You really don't know what's written there?" he said incredulously. "And I don't suppose dear Gerald knows either?"
"No, sir. No idea."

---

incredulous – ungläubig

"Michael... Alex... Can either of you tell me what it says on the other side of the blackboard?" "No, sir!" shouted the other two boys in chorus. Grimble reached forward and his fingers seized an ear. He drew this ear, together with the attached schoolboy, slowly towards him and said in his kindest, softest voice: "Very well. I'll only punish the one who has been telling lies. Run along, you three. You may join your friends in the playground!"

Which boy had been telling lies?

---

to seize	– ergreifen
with the attached schoolboy	– mit dem Schüler daran

4 The Laxton Motor Cycle Grand Prix

There were still thirteen hours to go before the start of the Laxton Grand Prix. This was one of the most important races for motor cycles of all classes, for single machines as well as for those with sidecars.

The beautiful summer weather had attracted thousands of fans to Laxton, and many of them had pitched their tents or parked their caravans within sight of the track. Even now, at eleven o'clock at night, the excitement about the place had not come to a stop. And if you listened hard, you could hear some bathers splashing about in the River Laxton, which gave its name to the course.

Fantastic speeds had been recorded during the day's practice runs, and two makes of motorbikes were favourites, Kamaki and Jonaface. Both firms were competing for the first time at the Laxton

---

the Laxton Grand Prix	– der Große Preis von Laxton
to attract	– anlocken
to pitch	– aufschlagen
within sight	– in Sichtweite
practice runs	– Probeläufe
make	– hier: Fabrikat, Marke
to compete	– teilnehmen

Grand Prix.
By now, everything was quiet in the pits where the teams were keeping a strict watch on their machines. The only ones where lights were still burning were those of the Suzuki, the Grand Decco and the Kamaki teams, and also in the Jonaface team, 200 metres upstream. But even here, by twenty minutes past midnight, all was dark and still.
Tom Hardy of Kamaki sat leaning against a wall, trying to fight his sleepiness. He looked at his watch. It was exactly three o'clock in the morning, and there was still an hour to go before Mike Sylvester would relieve him, the same Mike who lay beside him on a camp-bed, sleeping peacefully with a smile on his face. Tom Hardy was thinking about Bill, his ten-year-old son, who had had his appendix out the day before, and was very disappointed that he couldn't even watch the race on television. And in his mind, Tom Hardy began writing a letter to him...
Dear Bill,
I'm writing you this letter to keep myself awake. Remember, I've never written to you before. Until now we've always been together, and we could say

---

the pits	– die Boxen
to keep a strict watch on	– streng bewachen
to relieve	– ablösen
appendix	– Blinddarm
in his mind	– in seiner Vorstellung, in Gedanken

what we wanted to whenever we liked.
Today was the last practice day and we've come out of it pretty well. As you know, it's our first year here at Laxton. During the practice runs, our team had the second fastest time. I ought to feel pleased about this, and so I do... But what worries me is that the Jonaface machines were faster than ours and it's their first time here as well... You should have seen the face of their chief mechanic, Steve Miller, as he strutted about afterwards, pleased as Punch. Of course, I soon let him know we'd still got a trick or two up our sleeves. I only hope Meko Tabalis, our star rider, won't let us down. As you can see, Bill, it isn't always easy not to feel jealous... I've seen things happen so often, you know. There's a fellow here... He's riding for Gran Decco. I can't think of his name for the moment... Actually, I'm awfully tired, Bill, more than ready for bed...
Slowly Tom's head drooped forward, and then his deep even breathing showed that he had fallen asleep.
Ten minutes passed... Suddenly Tom Hardy

---

to strut	– stolzieren, schreiten
pleased as Punch	– stolz wie Oskar, überaus stolz
a trick or two up our sleeves	– noch ein paar Tricks in Reserve
to let down	– enttäuschen
jealous	– eifersüchtig
to droop	– herabhängen lassen

started. His tiredness fell away at once. There it was again, the same metallic click. There was no doubt about it. Someone was interfering with the machines.

Silently Hardy shook Mike Sylvester awake, got softly to his feet and reached for the light-switch. In doing so he fell over a can, and this gave the intruder an advantage of some seconds.

By the time the light came on, Tom was just able to see a pair of legs in yellow trousers disappearing through an airshaft. He ran outside and when he got to the end of the wall he saw the intruder's

---

to start – aufschrecken
doubt – Zweifel
intruder – Eindringling
airshaft – Luftschacht

shadow hurrying towards the river. Then the darkness swallowed him up.
Hardy ran back. Mike Sylvester was waiting inside and without a word he held out a piece of yellow material. And with a grim smile on his face, he said: “Gran Decco!”
Half an hour later, there was no one still asleep in the Kamaki camp. As well as the mechanics, there were the managers, the race organizers and, at last, the police. But Inspector Morris seemed to be the only one to keep his head.
The Inspector first sent for the three mechanics from Gran Decco and took them to another room.
“There can be no doubt that this piece of material comes from a pair of overalls used by your company.”
“That's nonsense,” replied the chief mechanic, Rodrina, with a laugh. “Do you really believe it's woven for Gran Decco only?”
And his colleague, Ramirez, added angrily: “It's all a frame-up. I shouldn't be surprised if it isn't just a publicity gag of Kamaki's!”
Rodrina and the third mechanic, Cortez, nodded.
“You can tell there's something fishy going on.

---

overall	– Arbeitshose
chief mechanic	– Chef-Mechaniker
to weave (wove, woven)	– weben
frame-up	– Komplott, abgekartetes Spiel
fishy	– verdächtig, ‚faul‘

Did you know some of our overalls have been stolen? And without them you can't prove we've got to do with it in any way."
Inspector Morris looked at Juan Cortez. "What were you doing at three o'clock?"
The man hesitated. "What do you mean? I was with the others. I wasn't anywhere near the river. I was in the pits."
"And what about you?" asked the Inspector, turning to Ramirez.
"I was in the pits, too. Rodrina is my witness that I didn't go out until all this began."
"Is that right, Mr Rodrina?"
"Yes, it's true."
"So none of you got any sleep? You were all awake?"
There was a moment's silence before Rodrina answered: "We took it in turns to sleep."
At this moment the door opened and a slight figure came in. In his left hand he held a fishing rod, and from his right one dangled a wet bundle. "I was told to give this to an Inspector Morris," he said in a grumbling voice.

---

to hesitate	– zögern
witness	– Zeuge
in turns	– abwechselnd
slight	– schächtig, dünn
to dangle	– baumeln
bundle	– Bündel
grumbling	– mürrisch

The Inspector took the bundle from him and opened it out on the floor. It was a pair of yellow overalls, with a piece torn out of one leg. The scrap which Inspector Morris held in his hand fitted in exactly. "Where did you get this, Mr...?"
"Cockney's the name, Jack Cockney. I've just fished it out of the river, behind the Jonaface pits..."
"And when was this?"
The man thought for a moment. "Something between three and half past. I'd arrived a few minutes before and was getting ready to throw my line when this came floating by, caught on a piece of driftwood. It was coming from the direction of the Kamaki paddock."
"Are you always up and about so early?" asked Inspector Morris.
At this, a broad smile came on Mr Cockney's face. "It's Nelson I'm after. At least, I've christened it Nelson: the biggest pike you've ever seen. I nearly caught it once, but I was out of luck and it got away..."
Juan Cortez jumped to his feet and pointed to the dripping overall. "Do you know what, Inspector? It must be the work of the Kamaki's themselves.

---

scrap – Fetzen
to christen – taufen
pike – Hecht

Anyone else would have made sure that this overall sank."
The Inspector smiled a little. "At night, it's almost impossible to see even a floating branch, you know."
At that moment Onega Kamaki himself appeared in the doorway. "Four of our machines have been sabotaged," he shouted angrily. "Have you found the culprit yet, Inspector?"
Morris took a deep breath. "I know that someone is telling lies," he answered slowly. "Whether the liar is also the culprit, or if the two are working hand in hand I have yet to find out, Mr Kamaki. But we're already hot on the trail!"

Who has been telling lies to Inspector Morris?

---

to be hot on the trail – eine heiße Spur haben

5 The forged banknote

Joe Gruber, the night porter at the Bear Hotel, put down his pen with an expression of satisfaction and murmured proudly: "Finished!"

That was what he always said whenever he had solved the crossword puzzle in the evening paper. It was a quarter to two in the morning. And since all the hotel rooms were taken, and all the guests had already gone to bed, he hoped he would have a peaceful night.

For a moment Joe pondered and then decided to prepare his accounts so that they were ready to hand over to the day porter when he arrived at seven o'clock. After that he would go through the list of early-morning calls and then he could safely settle down and take a nap.

Twenty minutes later, he had finished his paperwork and added everything up. All he had to do now was to make sure that he had 631 Marks in the till. He was putting the banknotes on a neat pile when he gave a start. There was no doubt

---

forged	– gefälscht
satisfaction	– Zufriedenheit
to ponder	– nachdenken
accounts	– Abrechnung
to take a nap	– ein Nickerchen machen

about it. One of the five one hundred Mark notes was noticeably different from the others: the colouring was several shades darker.
Completely baffled, Joe shook his head. How could he have failed to see it before? Quickly, he got a magnifying glass from the drawer and scrutinized the note for the watermark... And his hands were trembling with rage when a few moments later he picked up the telephone.
After half an hour of anxious waiting, at last the night-bell rang and Joe Gruber hurried to open the door.
The two gentlemen who followed him inside didn't look very pleased at being called at such an hour. The shorter of the two, who introduced himself as Inspector Horn, seemed particularly troubled about losing his sleep. "This is our technical expert, Dr Weinberg," he said, introducing his companion and he added yawning: "Scientists can manage with less sleep than us ordinary people, so he's wider awake than I am!"

---

noticeably	– auffällig
colouring	– Farbgebung
baffled	– verwirrt
to fail to see	– übersehen
magnifying glass	– Vergrößerungsglas
to scrutinize	– untersuchen
watermark	– Wasserzeichen
scientist	– Wissenschaftler
to manage	– hier: auskommen

Dr Weinberg smiled. "Don't worry about disturbing us, Mr..."
"Gruber's the name, Joe Gruber," said the porter.
"Well, Mr Gruber, where's the forged note you told us about?"
The porter took the five one hundred Mark notes from the till and spread them out on the counter. Without the slightest hesitation, the scientist picked out the darker note and handed it to Inspector Horn. "From the Dutch gang, don't you agree?"
The inspecotr nodded. "Yes, one of the same sort that turned up in Berlin, I'd say." And to the porter he said: "As you suspected, Mr Gruber, this is a forgery and not a very good one at that. So you were right to call us. I guess you don't know who planted it on you?"
"I certainly didn't notice it at the time, but it can only come from one of three gentlemen, who haven't yet left the hotel."
The inspector could hardly believe his ears. "I hope you're not trying to be funny!"
"No, no – I'm serious. This evening I've taken 631 Marks in cash. Most of it was for various odds and

---

gang	– Bande
at that	– obendrein
to plant on	– jemandem ‚andrehen'
in cash	– in bar, Bargeld
odds and ends	– Kleinigkeiten

ends like newspapers, stamps and postcards. The rest came from three of the customers who are leaving on the five a.m. train, and so have already paid their bills. Mr Korner's was 124 Marks, Mr Baukelius paid 219, and Mr van Straaten's came to 274 Marks."

"And all three gave you one hundred Mark notes?"

Without hesitation Gruber answered: "Yes, I've a good memory when it comes to money. Mr Kor-

---

bill – Rechnung

ner gave me one of the hundreds, plus some small change. The other two gentlemen each handed me two one hundred Mark notes, and the rest in smaller notes and coins. But I really can't understand why the difference in the colouring didn't stare me in the face."

Inspector Horn pointed to one of the three names in the list. "Which room is this man occupying?"

Joe looked at the bill and then at the police officer. "Do you honestly think he's the man?"

"If the culprit really is one of the three, he must be. Actually, you've been most helpful, Mr Gruber. It was one remark of yours that gave me the clue. You know, Dr Weinberg, I shan't be at all surprised if we find a few more of these forgeries in his luggage. Well, what's his room number?"

"It's 112, Inspector..."

Which of the visitors paid with the forged one hundred Mark note?

---

to stare in the face	–	ins Auge springen, auffallen
honestly	–	ehrlich, wirklich
clue	–	(entscheidender) Hinweis; Lösung

6 Gentleman Jim

For the third time within five minutes the expensive dark blue limousine drove almost noiselessly into Cedar Street and along the elegant villas, each of which radiated an air of luxury and wealth. Behind the wrought-iron railings were wonderful lawns and beds with exotic flowers. This was the kind of residential area where James Baker preferred to work, James Baker who was better known in professional circles as Gentleman Jim.

It was just before eleven o'clock at night.

After the fourth drive past, Baker believed he had found the ideal house for him. There was no light showing and the garage door was open.

He parked his car in the next road and then approached the villa of his choice.

No one would have guessed that the immaculate

---

to radiate	– ausstrahlen
air of luxury	– Hauch von Luxus
wrought-iron railings	– schmiedeeiserne Gitter
lawn	– Rasen
residential area	– Villenviertel
professional circles	– Fachkreisen
to approach	– sich nähern
choice	– Wahl
immaculate	– makellos

gentleman in full evening-dress, with an elegant cape, white silk scarf and gloves, was really an expert burglar.
Gentleman Jim was acknowledged in his field, even if, from time to time, he had seen the inside of a number of prisons in Europe.
By eighteen minutes past eleven he had succeeded in forcing a door open and stood listening in the hall of the villa he had decided to rob. The place seemed to be as empty as he had hoped it would be.
Gentleman Jim got down to work. Systematically he searched every room, beginning with those on the ground floor. His thoroughness was astonishing and his flair for finding the most rewarding drawers, cupboards and secret doors was second to none.
Before long his hands were full. He had two necklaces, some cuff-links, a platinum brooch and a purse with a great amount of money. With a bored air he dropped the articles into a pocket. Gentle-

---

silk scarf	– seidener Schal
to acknowledge	– anerkennen
to force open	– aufbrechen
thoroughness	– Gründlichkeit
flair	– Spürsinn, Instinkt
rewarding	– lohnend
second to none	– unvergleichlich
cuff-links	– Manschettenknöpfe
with a bored air	– gelangweilt

man Jim was after bigger loot than this.

Then he came to a room that could only have been a study. And with the assurance of a burglar who

---

loot – Beute
assurance – Selbstsicherheit

knows his craft he at once found the small wall-safe, which had a high-security lock. As he knew that he would find such a lock only where there is something valuable to hide he set to work immediately. Under his big cape he had a whole arsenal of precision instruments. But the minutes ticked by without success and Gentleman Jim grew impatient. Never before had he had to spend so much time on a wretched lock, and he became more and more furious with that person who had designed it.

James Baker wiped a few drops of sweat from his forehead, took off his gloves and placed them on a chair. Again and again he tried and finally, long after midnight, he succeeded at last. With a very faint click the levers yielded. Gentleman Jim opened the safe door and gave a cry of delight.

Before him, on a bed of red velvet, there glittered a number of jewels whose value could hardly be assessed. He sighed with pleasure and helped himself, stowing away the jewels inside his pockets as carefully as if he were handling new-laid eggs.

---

craft	– Handwerk
high-security lock	– Spezialsicherheitsschloß
wretched	– elend, verflixt
to design	– entwickeln, entwerfen
lever	– Bolzen
to yield	– nachgeben
velvet	– Samt
value	– Wert
to assess	– abschätzen

Then he froze in his tracks. No doubt, there was someone opening the front door. He slipped his torch into his cape and ran to the window.
By the time the owner of the house had reached the study James Baker had long since vanished. Only an open window showed that Gentleman Jim had been there.
Fifteen minutes later the police were on the spot and within an hour they were able to arrest the daring burglar. He had stopped at a filling-station for petrol, and the attendant, who had been listening to the radio, had no difficulty at all in recognizing him from the detailed description given by the police.
Although James Baker denied everything, the police could easily prove his guilt. One piece of evidence more than any other made everything clear for them.

What was the piece of evidence overlooked by Gentleman Jim?

---

to freeze in one's track	– wie festgewurzelt stehenbleiben
on the spot	– zur Stelle
daring	– wagemutig
attendant	– (Tankstellen-)Bedienung
to recognize	– erkennen
to deny	– leugnen
piece of evidence	– Beweisstück

7 True or false?

It was pouring hard on a cold October morning. Inspector Courtney looked at his watch and then stared out of the window. Nine o'clock and raining cats and dogs. Oh, for a cigarette! But his doctor had told him to give up smoking except on special occasions...

Dash it all, thought the inspector. Nine o'clock and a morning like this – didn't that make it a special occasion? Yes, it did!

It was after the third puff that he pressed the red button under his desk and a policeman came in.

"You rang, sir?" he asked.

"Yes. Send in that young man."

He disappeared and a few moments later a young man was shown in. His appearance was rather grubby and his manners rough. He didn't wait to be asked to sit down but flopped into a chair. "How much longer must I hang around? I can't

---

to rain cats and dogs	– sehr stark regnen, schütten
except on special occasions	– außer bei besonderen Gelegenheiten
dash it all!	– verflixt!
appearance	– Erscheinung, Äußeres
grubby	– schmuddelig, schlampig
manners	– Betragen
to flop	– sich plumpsen lassen

mess about here all day!"
The inspector took another puff and then said mildly: "Good morning, Mr Frink."
Adam Frink watched him suspiciously. Then he took a deep breath and began again: "Let me tell you that..."

---

to mess about – herumpfuschen, -treiben

"*I'm* doing the talking here, young man," the inspector interrupted him. "Sergeant Byng tells me that at twenty-five minutes to twelve last night you were caught in the act of..." – here he cleared his throat – "...of leaving number four Louisa Street by the cellar window. An awkward exit, isn't? Besides, the house belongs to Mr Scamp, and although Mr Scamp may come and go through his own cellar window whenever he wants, you, young man, are not Mr Scamp..."
After this rather long introduction, the police inspector returned to his cigarette, taking little notice of the fact that Frink had jumped up and was shaking his fists. "It's all a mistake, Inspector!" he shouted. "I wanted to give the family a surprise. The Scamps are friends of mine..."
Inspector Courtney seemed absorbed in blowing smoke-rings. Then he said: "Hm." A little later, he said "Hm" again. Another pause, this time followed by: "Tell me, do you always visit your friends through their cellar windows?"
"It was intended as a surprise! I've been trying to explain to the sergeant, but policemen are so stu-

---

to clear one's throat	–	sich räuspern
awkward	–	komisch, eigenartig
introduction	–	Einleitung
to give a surprise	–	überraschen
to be absorbed	–	in Gedanken verloren sein
to intend	–	beabsichtigen

pid they only understand words of one syllable."
"Of course, of course. It *is* sometimes difficult to explain things to them! So you wanted to give the Scamps a surprise?"
"Exactly. I'd no idea they were away. But when I got there I realized immediately there was no one in, so I turned back right away. I didn't even get as far as the kitchen. That's the truth!"
"The truth?"
"Yes, nothing but the truth."
"An interesting version," said the inspector smiling. "I see from your statement that you said you are a student."
"That's right."
"And what exactly are you studying?"
"At the moment I'm having a break." Mr Frink shrugged his shoulders. "Until last term, I was doing languages."
"Ancient or modern?"
"What d'you mean, ancient or modern? I was talking about foreign languages."
"Of course." Inspector Courtney stubbed out his cigarette. "When did you actually discover that the Scamps had gone away?"
"Oh, it was three days ago... quite by accident. I

---

to realize	– bemerken
term	– Semester
ancient	– alt(ertümlich)
by accident	– zufällig

was talking to someone and he said..."
"Do you remember the time you entered the house?"
From his reaction, one would have thought that Adam Frink was trying hard to get all the details right. "Of course I know what time it was. Ten o'clock precisely. The church clock was striking the hour. You couldn't help hearing it."
"One last question, Mr Frink. Sergeant Byng tells me you left the fridge door open in the kitchen. Did you?"
Adam Frink shook his head. "Sergeant Byng is mistaken," he exclaimed. "I'm certain I closed it. I remember slamming it."
"Splendid!" said the inspector, as if this were just the answer he wanted. "That's all for now. You may go."
"I can go?"
"Yes, back to your cell. Now I know you're just a common burglar. It never pays to tell lies, young man."
"What do you mean, lies?"
"It's quite simple. I've caught you lying not only once but three times. All I can say is that you ought to be ashamed of yourself."

---

common – gewöhnlich
it never pays – es zahlt sich nie aus

And for the second time that morning, Inspector Courtney pressed the red button under his desk.

What were the three lies which Adam Frink told?

Solutions

The man in black, page 7
The visitor who only pretended he'd been robbed was Mr Stan Simpson. The burglar could not get to his room, because the rope-ladder only reached down as far as the fourth floor. Mr Simpson's room, however, was below Frau Treicher's on the third floor. So the burglar could not have entered his room at all.

The rehearsal, page 29
The thief must have been the commissionaire, Mr Hart. If he really hadn't left the street entrance all morning, how could he have seen the messenger searching through coats and hats in the first-floor cloakroom?

Grimble is daft!, page 34
It was Michael Cash who gave himself away when he showed that he knew the words on the blackboard were written in *red* chalk.

The Laxton Motor Cycle Grand Prix, page 38
The fisherman was telling lies. Anything thrown into a river drifts downstream, not upstream. The Jonaface pits were 200 metres upstream from the Kamaki camp, so the bundle must have been thrown in the river near the Jonaface pits and could not have come floating from the direction described by Jack Cockney. The fisherman must have been paid by Jonaface, the rival team.

The forged banknote, page 46
In this case, the culprit can only be Mr Korner for he was the only one of the three who paid with a *single* one hundred Mark note. Inspector Horn realized this when Joe Gruber remarked: "But I really can't understand why the difference

in the colouring didn't stare me in the face." It would have done if he had got two notes together, one a forgery and the other genuine.

Gentleman Jim, page 51
Even an "expert" burglar makes mistakes. Gentleman Jim forgot his white gloves. And in his case they were as good as leaving a visiting card with his full name and address. Also, as he did not use his gloves he must have left his fingerprints on the wall-safe.

True or false?, page 56
Lie 1 Frink stated first that he didn't even know the Scamps were away. Then he said he had found this out three days before;
Lie 2 He entered the house at 10 p.m. and was arrested at 11.35 p.m. Therefore he did not leave again immediately, as he stated;
Lie 3 First he said that he hadn't got as far as the kitchen. Later he said that he hadn't left the fridge door open, but the fridge was, of course, in the kitchen.

---

downstream	–	flußabwärts
single	–	einzelne(r)
genuine	–	echt
to state	–	aussagen

Vocabulary

A to be absorbed [əb'zɔ:bd) – in Gedanken verloren sein

by accident ['æksidənt] – zufällig
accomplice [ə'kɔmplis] – Komplize
accounts [ə'kaunts] – Abrechnung
to acknowledge [ək'nɔlidʒ] – anerkennen
advantage [əd'vɑ:ntidʒ] – Vorteil
to take ~ of – seinen Nutzen ziehen aus
agony ['ægəni] – Qual, Pein
airshaft ['ɛəʃɑ:ft] – Luftschacht
alternative [ɔ:l'tə:nətiv] – Möglichkeit, Alternative
ancient ['einʃənt] – alt(ertümlich)
angelic [æn'dʒelik] – engelhaft, gleich
annoy [ə'nɔi] – (ver)ärgern
appalled [ə'pɔ:ld] – entsetzt
appearance [ə'piərəns] – Erscheinung, Äußeres
appendix [ə'pendiks] – Blinddarm
appointment [ə'pɔintmənt] – Verabredung, Termin
to approach [ə'prəutʃ] – sich nähern
to arouse [ə'rauz] – erwecken, wachrufen
arsenal ['ɑ:sinl] – Arsenal, Vorrat
to assess [ə'ses] – ab-, einschätzen
assistance [ə'sistəns] – Hilfe
assistant chef [ə'sistəntʃef] – stellvertr. Küchenchef
to assume [ə'sju:m] – annehmen, machen (Miene) aufsetzen
assurance [ə'ʃuərəns] – Selbstsicherheit
to assure [ə'ʃuə] – versichern
to attach [ə'tætʃ] – befestigen, beifügen
attendant [ə'tendənt] – (Tankstellen-) Bedienung

attentive [ə'tentiv] – aufmerksam
to attract [ə'trækt] – anlocken
to avoid [ə'vɔid] – vermeiden
awkward ['ɔːkwəd] – komisch, eigenartig

B baffled [bæfld] – verwirrt
to beam [biːm] – strahlen
to beat about the bush [buʃ] – um den heißen Brei herumreden
to behave [bi'heiv] – sich verhalten, betragen
belongings [bi'lɔŋiŋz] – Habseligkeiten
bewildered [bi'wildəd] – bestürzt
bill [bil] – Rechnung
to blackmail ['blækmeil] – erpressen
blame [bleim] – Schmach, Schande, Schuld
bored [bɔːd] – gelangweilt
break-in [breik in] – Einbruch
breath [breθ] – Atem
breeze [briːz] – Brise, sanfter Wind
briefcase ['briːfkeis] – Aktentasche
bundle [bʌndl] – Bündel
to burgl [bəːrgl] – bestehlen
to burst [bəːst] – brechen, stürmen
business ['biznis] – Geschäft, Angelegenheit

C to call on [kɔːl ɔn] – bei jemand vorsprechen
caretaker ['kɛəteikə] – Aufseher, Verwalter, Notenwart
case ['keis] – Fall, Schachtel
in cash [kæʃ] – in bar
cash register ['kæʃ'redʒistə) – Kasse
cat burglar ['kætbəːglə] – Fassadenkletterer, Einsteigdieb

cause [kɔːs]	– Grund, Ursache
caution ['kɔːʃn]	– Vorsicht, Verwarnung
quite by chance [tʃɑːns]	– ganz zufällig
to charge [tʃɑːdʒ]	– angreifen
choice [tʃɔis]	– Wahl
to christen ['krisn]	– taufen, nennen
circus performer ['səːkəs pə'fɔːmə]	– Artist
cloakroom ['kləukrum]	– Garderobe
clue [kluː]	– Hinweis, Lösung
coincidence [kəu'insidəns]	– Zufall, Zusammentreffen
to collide [kə'laid]	– zusammenstoßen
colouring ['kʌleriŋ]	– Farbgebung
comfortable ['kʌmfətəbl]	– bequem
commissionaire [kəmiʃə'nɛə]	– Portier
companion [kəm'pænjən]	– Begleiter
to compete [kəm'piːt]	– teilnehmen
composition [kɔmpə'ziʃn]	– Aufsatz
conductor [kən'dʌktə]	– Dirigent
to confess [kən'fes]	– bekennen, zugeben
considerable [kən'sidərəbl]	– beträchtlich
to console [kən'səul]	– trösten
contrary ['kɔntrəri]	– Gegenteil
conviction [kən'vikʃən]	– Überzeugung
co-operate [kəu'ɔpəreit]	– zusammenarbeiten
to cover up ['kʌvər 'ʌp]	– verwischen
craft [krɑːft]	– Handwerk
crook [kruk]	– hier: Gauner, Betrüger
fellow ~	Gegenspieler, konkurrierender Gauner
to cross-examine ['krɔs ig'zæmin]	– ins Kreuzverhör nehmen
cubbyhole ['kʌbihəul]	– Raum, „Kabuff“
cuff-link ['kʌf-link]	– Manschettenknopf
culprit ['kʌlprit]	– Übeltäter, Schuldiger
curious ['kjuəriəs]	– neugierig

D	daft [dɑːft]	– doof, blöd
	to dangle [dæŋgl]	– baumeln
	daring [dɛəriŋ]	– wagemutig
	dash it all [dæʃ]	– verflixt
	defiant [di'faiənt]	– verächtlich
	to defraud [di'frɔːd]	– betrügen
	to deliver [di'livə]	– abgeben, überbringen
	to deny [di'nai]	– leugnen, abstreiten
	to design [di'zain]	– entwickeln, entwerfen
	devastating ['devəsteitiŋ]	– verheerend
	to dial ['daiəl]	– wählen (Telefon)
	disaster [di'zɑːstə]	– Katastrophe
	to discover [dis'kʌvəri]	– entdecken
	discovery [dis'kʌvəri]	– Entdeckung
	display case [dis'pleikeis]	– Schaukasten
	to disturb [dis'təːb]	– stören
	doubt [daut]	– Zweifel
	downstream ['daunstriːm]	– flußabwärts
	drawer [drɔːə]	– Schublade
	dreadful ['dredful]	– fürchterlich, schlimm
	dressmaker ['dresmeikə]	– Schneider(in)
	to droop [druːp]	– herabhängen lassen
	to drop in on [drɔp]	– jemanden überraschend besuchen
	duty ['djuːti]	– Pflicht, Dienst
	off ~	– dienstfrei
E	eager ['iːgə]	– begierig
	efficient [i'fiʃənt]	– wirkungsvoll
	to eliminate [i'limineit]	– ausschließen
	to embarrass [im'bærəs]	– verwirren
	emergency [i'məːdʒənsi]	– Notfall
	~ exit	– Notausgang
	to employ [im'plɔi]	– beschäftigen
	entire(ly) [in'taiə]	– ganz, gänzlich
	evidence ['evidəns]	– Zeugnis, Beweis
	except [ik'sept]	– außer

	to exclaim [iks'kleim]	– ausrufen
	expression [iks'preʃn]	– (Gesichts)Ausdruck
F	to fail [feil]	– keinen Erfolg haben mit
	faint [feint]	– schwach
	festive ['festiv]	– feierlich, festlich
	fingerprint ['fiŋgə print]	– Fingerabdruck
	fire extinguisher ['faiər‿ iks'tiŋgwiʃə]	– Feuerlöscher
	fishy ['fiʃi]	– verdächtig, 'faul'
	to fix [fiks]	– befestigen
	flair [flɛə]	– Spürsinn, Instinkt
	to flake away [fleik ə'wei]	– abblättern
	fleeting ['fli:tiŋ]	– flüchtig
	to flop [flɔp]	– sich plumpsen (fallen) lassen
	to force open [fɔ:s]	– aufbrechen
	to forge [fɔ:dʒ]	– fälschen
	frame-up ['freim ʌp]	– Komplott, abgekartetes Spiel
	to freeze [fri:z]	– frieren, festfrieren
	French window ['frentʃ 'windou]	– Verandatür
	fridge [fridʒ] (= refrigerator)	– Kühlschrank
	to frown [fraun]	– die Stirn runzeln
	fruitless ['fru:tləs]	– fruchtlos, nutzlos
	further ['fə:ðə]	– weitere
G	gang [gæŋ]	– Bande
	to gasp [gɑ:sp]	– nach Luft schnappen
	genuine ['dʒenjuin]	– echt
	to make the get away	– abhauen
	to get rid of	– loswerden
	to give oneself away	– sich verraten
	to gleam [gli:m]	– funkeln, strahlen

gloves [glʌvz] – Handschuhe
greedy ['gri:di] – gierig
grocery warehouse ['grousəri] – Lebensmittellager, ~ Großmarkt
to grope for [grəup] – tasten, suchen nach
grubby ['grʌbi] – schmuddelig
grumbling ['grʌmbliŋ] – mürrisch
to be on the guard [gɑ:d] – auf der Hut sein
guilt [gilt] – Schuld
guilty ['gilti] – schuldig

H haste [heist] – Eile
headaches ['hedeiks] – Kopfschmerzen
health [helθ] – Gesundheit
hesitate ['heziteit] – zögern
high-security ['hai si'kjuriti] – besonders sichere(r)
hoarse [hɔ:s] – heiser
hollow ['hɔlou] – hohl
in the ~ of the hand – völlig i. d. Hand, Gewalt
honestly ['ɔnistli] – ehrlich, wirklich
horrified ['hɔrifaid] – entsetzt
to huddle [hʌdl] – sich zusammendrängen

I identity [ai'dentiti] – Identität, wer jemand ist
to imagine [i'mædʒin] – sich vorstellen
immaculate [i'mækjulit] – makellos, untadelig
impatient [im'peiʃənt] – ungeduldig
impertinent [im'pə:tinənt] – unverschämt
incredulous [in'kredjuləs] – ungläubig
innocent ['inəsənt] – unschuldig
inquisitive [in'kwizitiv] – neugierig
to insist [in'sist] – bestehen auf
insurance [in'ʃuərəns] – Versicherung
to intend [in'tend] – beabsichtigen

	to interfere [intə'fiə]	– sich einmischen
	to interject [intə'dʒekt]	– einwerfen, unterbrechen
	to interrogate [in'terəgeit]	– verhören, befragen
	to interrupt [intə'rʌpt]	– unterbrechen
	to intervene [intə'vi:n]	– dazwischentreten
	to introduce ['intrədju:s]	– vorstellen
	introduction [intrə'dʌkʃən]	– Einleitung
	intruder [in'tru:də]	– Eindringling
	investigation [investi'geiʃn]	– Untersuchung
	to involve [in'vɔlv]	– verwickeln, beteiligen
J	jealous ['dʒeləs]	– eifersüchtig
	jeweller ['dʒu:ələ]	– Juwelier
	joint [dʒɔint]	– Kneipe, Lokal, „Laden"
	juvenile court ['dʒuvənail kɔ:t]	– Jugendgericht
K	keen on [ki:n]	– begierig, eifrig zu...
	to keep one's head [ki:p]	– einen kühlen Kopf behalten
	to keep in	– zum Nachsitzen dabehalten
	krone [krəun] (pl. kroner)	– Krone (skandinavische Währung)
L	landing ['lændiŋ]	– Treppenabsatz
	lapel ['leipəl]	– Rockaufschlag, Revers
	lawn [lɔ:n]	– Rasen
	to lean forward [li:n]	– sich vorbeugen
	to lean out [li:n]	– sich hinauslehnen
	leather ['leðə]	– (aus) Leder
	ledge [ledʒ]	– Sims
	to let down [let 'daun]	– allein lassen, enttäuschen
	lever ['li:və]	– Bolzen

	limousine ['limuzi:n]	– Limousine, Pkw
	local [ləukəl]	– örtlich, Orts-
	loot [lu:t]	– Beute
	loss [lɔs]	– Verlust
	to lower ['ləuə]	– herunterlassen
M	magnifying glass ['mægnifaiiŋ]	– Vergrößerungsglas
	make [meik]	– hier: Fabrikat, Marke
	to manage ['mænidʒ]	– hier: auskommen
	manners ['mænəz]	– Betragen
	mask [mɑ:sk]	– Maske
	mechanik [mi'kænik]	– Mechaniker
	to menace ['menis]	– (be)drohen
	to mess about [mes]	– herumpfuschen, treiben
	to mess up [mes 'ʌp]	– vermasseln, versauen
	minor ['mainə]	– gering, unbedeutend
	to mistrust [mis'trʌst]	– mißtrauen
	to mix up with [miks]	– verwechseln
	moonless ['mu:nlis]	– ohne Mond
	motionless ['məuʃnlis]	– bewegungslos
	music publishers ['mju:zik 'pʌbliʃəz]	– Musikverlag
	to mutter ['mʌtə]	– murmeln
N	(to take a) nap [næp]	– ein Nickerchen machen
	nimbly ['nimbli]	– gewandt, geschickt
	noticeably ['nəutisəbli]	– auffällig
O	oasis [əu'eiziz]	– Oase
	objection [əb'dʒekʃn]	– Einwand
	occasion [ə'keiʒən]	– Gelegenheit
	to occupy ['ɔkjupai]	– belegen, bewohnen
	odd [ɔd]	– komisch, eigenartig
	odds and ends [ɔdz]	– Kleinigkeiten

	offhand ['ɔfhænd]	– kurz angebunden
	ordinary ['ɔːdnri]	– gewöhnlich, normal
	outstanding [aut'stændiŋ]	– hervorragend
	overall ['əuvərɔːl]	– Arbeitshose, Monteuranzug
	to own [əun]	– besitzen
	to own up [əun'ʌp]	– ein Geständnis ablegen
P	pale [peil]	– blaß
	pane [pein]	– Scheibe
	to pat [pæt]	– hier: streichen über
	to pay [pei]	– bezahlen
	~ a visit	– einen Besuch abstatten
	performance [pə'fɔːməns]	– Werk, Tat
	pike [paik]	– Hecht
	pit [pit]	– Box, Kabine
	to pitch [pitʃ]	– aufschlagen
	to plant something on	– „andrehen“, loswerden an
	plaster ['plɑːstə]	– Gips, Außenputz
	to ponder [pɔndə]	– nachdenken
	posh [pɔʃ]	– todschick, pikfein
	practice run ['præktis rʌn]	– Proberennen, -lauf
	precious ['preʃəs]	– wertvoll
	to pretend [pri'tend]	– vortäuschen, so tun als ob
	probably ['prɔbəbli]	– vermutlich
	professional [prə'feʃənl]	– professionell, Fach ~
	to prolong [prə'lɔŋ]	– verlängern
	to prove [pruːv]	– beweisen
Q	to quicken ['kwikən]	– beschleunigen
R	to radiate ['reidieit]	– ausstrahlen, verbreiten

rage [reidʒ]	– Wut
railing ['reiliŋ]	– Gitter, Geländer
to reach [riːtʃ]	– (er)reichen
to realize ['riəlaiz]	– bemerken
reception [ri'sepʃn]	– Empfang
to recover [ri'kʌvə]	– wiederfinden
rehearsal [ri'həsl]	– (Orchester-)Probe
to relax [ri'læks]	– entspannen, hier: wieder atmen
relief ~ [ri'liːf]	– Aushilfs-
to relieve [ri'liːv]	– ablösen
reluctantly [ri'lʌktəntli]	– widerwillig
to remain [ri'mein]	– (ver)bleiben
remorseless [ri'mɔːslis]	– erbarmungslos
to repeat [ri'piːt]	– wiederholen
to replace [ri'pleis]	– auflegen, ersetzen
residential area [rezi'denʃəl]	– Villengegend
in that respect [ris'pekt]	– in dieser Hinsicht
restless ['restləs]	– ruhelos
result [ri'zʌlt]	– Ergebnis
retired [ri'taiəd]	– pensioniert
reward [ri'wɔːd]	– Belohnung
rewarding [ri'wɔːdiŋ]	– lohnend
rin [rim]	– Rand
ring [riŋ]	– hier: Unterton, Beiklang
rooted ['ruːtid]	– angewurzelt
rope ladder ['rəuplædə]	– Strickleiter
rough [rʌf]	– rauh, ungehobelt
rung [rʌŋ]	– Sprosse
S satisfaction [sætis'fækʃn]	– Befriedigung
scarf [skaːf]	– Schal
scientist ['saiəntist]	– Wissenschaftler
score [skɔː]	– Partitur, Notenbuch
to scowl at [skaul]	– finster anblicken
scrap [skræp]	– Fetzen

to scratch [skrætʃ]	– kratzen
to scrutinize ['skrutinaiz]	– untersuchen
to search [səːtʃ]	– (durch)suchen
second to none ['sekənd]	– unvergleichlich
to seize [siːz]	– (er)greifen, packen
self-possession ['self pə'zeʃn]	– Fassung
a big shot [ʃɔt]	– „großes Tier", Bonze
within sight [sait]	– in Sichtweite
silk [silk]	– Seide, seiden, seidig
sincere [sin'siə]	– ernst
single [siŋgl]	– einzelne(r)
to slam [slæm]	– zuknallen
up our sleeve [sliːv]	– in Reserve
slight [slait]	– schmächtig, dünn
slightly ['slaitli]	– leicht, ein wenig
to smash [smæʃ]	– einschlagen, zerbrechen
snore [snɔː]	– Schnarchen
to sob out [sɔb]	– hinaus seufzen
to solve [sɔlv]	– lösen
to spare [spɛə]	– übrig haben, erübrigen
to spin [spin]	– drehen, sich drehen
on the spot [spɔt]	– zur Stelle
springy ['spriŋi]	– federnd, elastisch
to succeed [sək'siːd]	– Erfolg haben
suit [sjuːt]	– Anzug
to (give a) surprise [sə'praiz]	– überraschen
to suspect [səs'pekt]	– vermuten
suspicious [səs'piʃəs]	– verdächtig
to swallow ['swɔləu]	– schlucken, verschlingen
(in full) swing [swiŋ]	– in vollem Gang
St staff lift [stɑːf lift]	– Personalaufzug
to stammer ['stæmə]	– stammeln
to stare (in the face) [stɛə]	– auffallen, ins Auge springen

to start [sta:t] – hier: aufschrecken
to state [steit] – aussagen
statement ['steitmənt] – Aussage
sticky tape ['stiki'teip] – Klebeband
string player ['striŋ 'pleiə] – Spieler eines Streichinstruments
to struggle for [strʌgl] – ringen nach
to strut [strʌt] – stolzieren, schreiten

T to tackle [tækl] – in Angriff nehmen, wagen
takings ['teikiŋz] – Einnahmen
to tap [tæp] – klopfen
tear [tiə] – Träne
to teeter ['ti:tə] – wanken, schaukeln
term [tə:m] – Semester, Halbjahr
terrify ['terifai] – erschrecken
thin (excuse) [θin] – dürftig (Entschuldigung)
thoroughness ['θʌrənis] – Gründlichkeit
to threaten [θretn] – (be)drohen
throat [θrəut] – Kehle
to clear one's ~ – sich räuspern
to tie up ['tai' ʌp] – festbinden
till [til] – Kasse
to totter ['tɔtə] – torkeln, schwanken
trace [treis] – Spur
trail [treil] – Spur, Fährte
trainee [trei'ni:] – Lehrling, Auszubildende(r)
trunk [trʌŋk] – großer Koffer
truth [tru:θ] – Wahrheit
to tune up ['tju:n'ʌp] – (ein)stimmen
to turn loose on [tə:n lu:s] – auf die Fährte setzen
to turn out as – sich herausstellen als

U unconvincing ['ʌnkən'vinsiŋ] – ohne Überzeugung

	unmistakable ['ʌnmis'teikəbl]	– klar, unmißverständlich
	upset [ʌp'set]	– ungehalten
	utmost ['ʌtməust]	– äußerst
V	valuable ['væljuəbl]	– wertvoll
	value ['vælju:]	– Wert
	various ['vɛəriəs]	– diverse, verschiedene
	velvet ['velvit]	– Samt
	victim ['viktim]	– Opfer
	villain ['vilən]	– Schurke
W	wallet ['wælit]	– Brieftasche
	warehouse ['wɛəhaus]	– Lagerhaus, Großmarkt
	warily ['wɛərili]	– vorsichtig, behutsam
	watermark ['wɔ:təmɑ:k]	– Wasserzeichen
	wealthy ['welθi]	– wohlhabend
	weary ['wiəri]	– müde
	to weave (wove, woven) [wi:v]	– weben
	witness ['witnis]	– Zeuge
	to wonder ['wʌndə]	– wissen mögen
	wretched ['retʃid]	– elend, verflixt
	wrought-iron ['rɔ:t'aiən]	– schmiedeeisern
Y	to yield [ji:ld]	– nachgeben

CLUB DER DETEKTIVE

Kriminalfälle zum Selberlösen von Wolfgang Ecke

Eine Serie mit Detektivgeschichten, die alle mit einer Frage enden. Wer war der Täter? Wodurch hat sich der Verdächtige verraten? Wer aufmerksam liest und mitdenkt, kommt auf die Lösung. Folgende Bände sind bisher erschienen:

Band 208 **Das Schloß der roten Affen**
Band 214 **Der Mann in Schwarz**
Band 221 **Das Gesicht an der Scheibe**
Band 227 **Solo für Melodica**
Band 264 **Das Geheimnis der alten Dschunke**
Band 306 **Das Haus der 99 Geister**
Band 315 **Erben auf schottisch**
Band 365 **Schach bei Vollmond**
Band 403 **Der unsichtbare Zeuge**
Band 650 **Ein Gauner spielte Mundharmonika**
Band 861 **Keine Spur von Paul Crabbley**

Ihr könnt einige dieser spannenden Detektivgeschichten auch auf englisch lesen. Das ist genauso spannend – und ganz nebenbei lernt man auch noch etwas Englisch dazu.

Band 560 **The Face at the Window**
Band 561 **The Man in Black**
Band 648 **The Secret of the Chinese Junk**
Band 718 **The House of the 99 Ghosts**

Ravensburger Taschenbücher ® Ravensburger

JEANS BÜCHER

Jeans-Bücher
kritisch · spannend · engagiert
Themen von heute
für die Erwachsenen von morgen

Bayer, Ingeborg
Noack, Hans-Georg
David und Dorothee
Zwei Jugendliche erzählen aus ihrem Leben
RTB 819 ab 14

Clavel, Bernhard
Nacht über Malataverne
Spannender Jugendkrimi
RTB 742 ab 14

Gabel, Wolfgang
Der Aufstieg der Familie Kohlbrenner
Eine Familiengeschichte
RTB 716 ab 13

Kirsch/Günther (Hrsg.)
Die beste aller möglichen Welten
Eine Anthologie
RTB 697 ab 14

Körner, Wolfgang
Der Weg nach drüben
In Deutschland zu Hause 1
RTB 709 ab 14

Körner, Wolfgang
Und jetzt die Freiheit
In Deutschland zu Hause 2
RTB 710 ab 14

Noack, Hans-Georg
Rolltreppe abwärts
Ein Ladendiebstahl und seine Folgen
RTB 299 ab 12

Noack, Hans-Georg
Trip
Über die Wirkung von Drogen
RTB 320 ab 12

Noack, Hans-Georg
Hautfarbe Nebensache
Rassendiskrimination im Alltag
RTB 696 ab 13

Pelot, Pierre
Gesucht wird
Ein Jugendkrimi
RTB 677 ab 14

Wyss, Hedi
Welt hinter Glas
Ein Mädchenbuch
RTB 760 ab 14

Wyss/Schaad (Hrsg.)
Rotstrumpf 3
Die Welt, die uns umgibt.
Anthologie für Mädchen
RTB 676 ab 13

Ravensburger Taschenbücher

Bücher von **Hans Jürgen Press**

Die Abenteuer der »schwarzen hand«

Ravensburger Taschenbücher Band 60

Diese rätselhaften Detektivgeschichten zum Mitraten zählen zu den beliebtesten in den Ravensburger Taschenbüchern.

Die Abenteuer der »schwarzen hand« sind auch in englischer Sprache erschienen:

The Black Hand Gang and the Mysterious House

Ravensburger Taschenbücher Band 504

The Black Hand Gang and the Treasure in Breezy Lake

Ravensburger Taschenbücher Band 505

Klassiker der Weltliteratur – Klassiker der Kinderliteratur

Charles Dickens OLIVER TWIST	Band 139
H. J. Chr. von Grimmelshausen DER ABENTEUERLICHE SIMPLICISSIMUS	Band 132
Wilhelm Hauff DAS GESPENSTERSCHIFF UND ANDERE GESCHICHTEN	Band 192
Hugh Lofting DOKTOR DOLITTLE UND SEINE TIERE	Band 153
Mark Twain DIE ABENTEUER DES HUCKLEBERRY FINN	Band 103
Mark Twain TOM SAWYERS ABENTEUER	Band 135
Edgar Allan Poe DIE DENKWÜRDIGEN ERLEBNISSE DES ARTUR GORDON PYM	Band 225

Nacherzählungen von Erich Kästner

DON QUICHOTTE	Band 543
DER GESTIEFELTE KATER	Band 522
GULLIVERS REISEN	Band 27
MÜNCHHAUSEN	Band 198
DIE SCHILDBÜRGER	Band 117
TILL EULENSPIEGEL	Band 172

Jack London erzählt

GOLDSUCHER	Band 603
DER RUF DER WILDNIS	Band 171
DER SEEWOLF	Band 577
WOLFSBLUT	Band 589